Acknowledgement of Land & of the Traditional Owners of this Land

I would like to acknowledge the Gadigal people of the Eora Nation, upon whose stolen land I stand on today.
I recognise that this land was never terra nullius — the land belonging to these peoples was never ceded, given up, bought or sold.
I would like to pay my respects to Aboriginal Elders past, present and emerging, and I extend this acknowledgement to all Aboriginal and Torres Strait Islander people.

When I Was Young

"The rooms were so much colder then
My father was a soldier then
And times were very hard
When I was young
I smoked my first cigarette at ten
And for girls, I had a bad yen
And I had quite a ball
When I was young.

When I was young, it was more important
Pain more painful
Laughter much louder
Yeah, when I was young
When I was young.

I met my first love at thirteen
She was brown and I was pretty green
And I learned quite a lot when I was young
When I was young.
When I was young.

Pain more painful
Laughter much louder
Yeah, when I was young
When I was young.

My faith was so much stronger then
I believed in fellow man
And I was so much older then
When I was young
When I was young
When I was young."

Songwriter: Eric Burdon

"Difesa"
My old farmhouse in Italy
Photo circa 1979

"The Young Don"
16 years young
Photo circa 1976

Contents

1: A Moment
(Un Momento)
2: She Has Always Been Alone
(È sempre Stata Sola)
3: I Feel Like a Puppy Dog
(Mi Sento un Cucciolo di Cane)
4: I Think I'm Becoming Brazilian
(Penso che sto Diventando Brasiliano)
5: Listen to Your HE♥RT
(Ascolta il tuo Cuore)
6: Calm Inside a Storm
(Calma Dentro una Tempesta)
7: Stay Calm
(Stai Calma)
8: Music is Gonna Save Us
(La Musica ci Salverà)
9: You've Gotta Take What You Get
(Devi Prendere Quello che Ottieni)
10: Don't Ask the Question
(Non Fare la Domanda)
11: The day the Universe Changed
(Il Giorno in cui l'Universo è Cambiato)
12: The Perfect Saturday Night
(Il Sabato Sera Perfetto di Sempre)
13: I Am in Prison
(Sono in Prigione)
14: Why?
Perché?
15: Where the streets Have No Names
(Dove le Strade Non Hanno Nome)
16: Be Shameless
(Senza Vergogna)
17: Come in From the Cold
(Vieni dal Freddo)

Contents

18: Do you Have the Courage?
(Hai il Coraggio?)
19: Calm Your Mind
(Calma la tua Mente)
20: Got you on My Mind
(Ti ho nella Mia Mente)
21: Wanted DEAD or ALIVE
(Ricercato VIVO o MORTO)
22: Why not?
(Perchè No?)
23: Happiness
(Oh Lord, Won't you Buy Me a Mercedes Benz)
(Felicità (Oh Signore non mi Comprerai una Mercedes Benz))
24: I Can't Stop Myself
(Io Non Mi Posso Fermare)
25: STOP!
(Fermare!)
26: Don't Worry, Be Happy
(Non Preoccuparti, Sii Felice)
27: Freedom (What Freedom?)
(Libertà (quale libertà?))
28: Don't!
(Non Farlo)
29: ACCEPT!
(Acceto)
30: Fascism Has Won!
(Il Fascismo ha Vinto!)
31: Watch & See
(Guadare e Vedere)
32: Don't FUCK Around with ME!
(Non Scopare in Giro con ME!)
33: Deconstruct
(Decostruire)
34: No Words Required
(Non Parole e Necessaria)

Contents

35: Protest!
(Protesta)
36: Hypocrisy
(Ipocrisia)
37: I Do Whatever the FUCK I Want!
(Faccio Tutto il CAZZO che Voglio)
38: Ghost Town
(Città Fantasma)
39: Fuck Like Animals
(Scopa Come gli Animali)
40: Don't Stay Safe
(Non Stare Al Sicuro)
41: Trouble Maker
(Piantagrane)
42: Remember, You Can Do Anything!
(Ricorda, Puoi Fare Qualsiasi Cosa!)
43: Narcissist
(Narcisista)
44: Voice of the Voiceless
(La Voce dei Senza Voce)
45: What Sort of Death Will You Have?
(Che Tipo di Morte Avrai?)
46: Eco-Warrior
(Eco-Guerriero)
47: What Kind of Drunk Are You?
(Che Tipo di Ubriaco Sei?)
48: When There is No Tomorrow
(Quando non c'è Domani)
49: Boundaries
(Confini)
50: Time
(Tempo)
51: Follow the RULES!
(Segui le Regole)

A Moment

(Un Momento)

A Moment.
That's all that's required.
A Moment.
To set things right.
A Moment.
To make things better.
A Moment.
To make your world bright.
A Moment.
To let in "The LIGHT".
A Moment.
To bring in the happiness.
A Moment.
To bring in the joy.
A Moment.
To satisfy your longing.
A Moment.
To quench you DESIRE.
A Moment.
To fulfill your PASSION.
A Moment.
To set you on FIRE.
A Moment is all that's required.
A Moment.
To make you feel.
A Moment.
To make you feel like a Human Being again.
A Moment....
...that's all that's required.
A Moment.
In "Space-Time".
A Moment.
That lasts a "Lifetime".

A Moment.
Of HOPE.
A Moment.
Of FAITH.
A Moment.
Of pure pleasure.
A Moment.
Of pure BLISS.
A Moment.
Of pure LO♥E.
A Moment.
Of pure ECSTASY.
A Moment.
An ETERNITY.

A single, solitary MOMENT...
...that's all that's required.
A Moment.

"The Don"
11.07.2021

She Has Always Been Alone
(È sempre Stata Sola)

She has never needed anyone.
She has done everything by herself.
She is a fighter.
She is a perfectionist.
She never gives up.
She has always struggled.
She has never relied on anyone else.
She is tough.
She does not *"suffer fools gladly"*.
She takes no prisoners.
She never looks back.
She has done this for 42 years.
She has always been alone.

But...
...life has taken its toll.
She is feeling weary.
She is feeling tired.
She is feeling exhausted.
She is stressed.
She is feeling alone.
For the first time in her life...
...she feels she might need someone.
Someone to...
...share her burden.
...share her load.
...help her carry her cross.
...the one she's been carrying for ALL of her life.
Because...
...she has always been alone.

"But maybe not anymore".
"If she'll let herself".

"The Don"
13.07.2021

I Feel Like a Puppy Dog

(Mi Sento un Cucciolo di Cane)

"I feel like a puppy dog when I'm around you."
"I just want to jump up & down."
"I just want to lick you."
"I just want to hump you."
"I know she says".
"All men do the same thing around me!"
"You are no different!"
"They all act like little puppies!"
"Don't feel too bad".
"I'm used to it."
"It's been happening all my life."
"I feel like a puppy dog when I'm around you."

I try to refrain myself.
I try to remember my credo...
..."maintain The VOID!"
..."Trust The VOID!"
But I can't stop myself.
I have no control.
I am weak.
I reprimand myself.
"STOP!"
"MAINTAIN The VOID!"
But to no avail.
It's useless.
I continue to...
...feel like a puppy dog when I'm around you!

"The Don"
13.07.2021

I Think I'm Becoming Brazilian

(Penso che sto Diventando Brasiliano)

I like to *PARTY!*
I like to *party ALL night long!*
I like to *SING!*
I like to *sing ALL night long!*
I like to *DANCE!*
I like to *dance ALL night long!*
I like to *RAGE!*
I like to *rage ALL night long!*
I like to *make ROMANCE!*
I like to *make romance ALL night long!*
I think I'm becoming Brazilian.

I have Brazilian music in my head.
I wake up with Brazilian music in my head.
I don't understand the words.
I don't have too.
Because...
...I understand the music.
...I understand the meaning.
...I feel it in my HE♥RT.
...I feel it in my SOUL.
...I feel it in my very BEING.
I think I'm becoming Brazilian.

The music moves me.
The music soothes me.
The music takes to another place.
The music takes me to another time.
The music takes me HIGH.
I think I'm becoming Brazilian.

"I'm a PARTY ANIMAL!"

"Maybe I was already Brazilian but didn't know it?"

"The Don"
14.07.2021

Listen to Your HE♥RT

(Ascolta il tuo Cuore)

Do you hear it?
Listen.
Do you feel it?
Feel.
It's speaking to you.
You know what it's saying.
You know what you have to do.
You know what you MUST do.
Listen to your HE♥RT.

It has the answers.
It has the solution.
It knows what you want.
It knows what you have to do.
It's speaking to you.
You know what it's saying.
You know what you have to do.
You know what you MUST do.
Listen to your HE♥RT.

You are in doubt.
You're not sure.
You are confused.
You can hear you HE♥RT.
But...
...it's your head.
...you are rationalising.
...you are questioning.
...should I, or shouldn't I?
Should I listen to my head or...
...listen to my HE♥RT?

Deep down inside you.
You know that you have to do...
...eventually.
...if you want to be HAPPY.
You can put it off.
You can't deny it.
Your HE♥RT is speaking to you.
Are you listening?
Are you hearing what it's saying?
You know what it's saying.
You know what you have to do.
You know what you MUST do.
Listen to your HE♥RT.

"The Don"
15.07.2021

Calm Inside a Storm

(Calma Dentro una Tempesta)

There's a storm a'raging.
It's taking everything in its path.
It's ravaging the land.
It's destroying our minds.
There is nowhere you can hide.
There is nowhere you can run to.
There is nowhere you can seek shelter.
There is nowhere you can find shelter from the storm.
There is no calm Inside a storm.

There is panic throughout the land.
There is fear in everyone's eyes.
There is the stench of DEATH in the air.
There is thunder in the sky.
There is lightning that is like electricity gone crazy.
There is a wind that is blowing a hurricane.
There is nothing you can do.
There is nowhere you can hide.
There is nowhere you can run to.
There is nowhere you can seek shelter.
You cannot seek shelter from this storm.
There is no calm Inside a storm.

"The Don"
15.07.2021

Stay Calm

(Stai Calma)

Don't *freak out*.
Don't *stress out*.
Don't *panic*.
Don't *"black out"*.
Don't *overthink*.
Don't *scream*.
Don't have a *"brain explosion"*.
Don't go *crazy*.
Don't go *mad*.
Don't go *"psycho"*.
Stay calm.

Stay *"cool"*.
Stay *"chilled"*.
Stay *relaxed*.
Stay *calm*.
Stay *positive*.
Stay *optimistic*.
Stay *happy*.
Stay *caring*.
Stay *kind*.
Stay *compassionate*.
Stay *affectionate*.
Stay LO♥ING.
Stay calm.

"You can cry if you want to, though!"

"Calma
Que eu já tô pensando no futuro
Que eu já tô driblando a madrugada
Não é tudo isso, é quase nada
Tempestade em copo d'água"

"Eu não tenho medo do escuro
Sei que logo vem a alvorada
Deixa a luz do Sol bater na estrada
Ilumina o asfalto negro
Oh, oh
Ilumina o asfalto negro
Oh, oh

Não faz assim
Não diga que não gosta de mim
Não diga que não vai me notar
No pé do bar em qualquer lugar
Não venha me dizer que não dá
Não quero ver você se perder
Não diga que não vai me mudar
Não diga que é difícil demais

Calma
Que eu já tô pensando no futuro
Que eu já tô driblando a madrugada
Não é tudo isso, é quase nada
Tempestade em copo d'água

Eu não tenho medo do escuro
Sei que logo vem a alvorada
Deixa a luz do Sol bater na estrada
Ilumina o asfalto negro
Oh, oh
Ilumina o asfalto negro
Oh, oh

Não faz assim
Não diga que não gosta de mim
Não diga que não vai me notar
No pé do bar em qualquer lugar
Não venha me dizer que não deu
Não diga que não vai me esquecer
Não diga que não sabe explicar
Eu juro que não dá pra entender."

"Calma...
Calma...
Calma...
Calma...

Calma...
Calma...
Calma...
Calma...

Ilumina o asfalto negro
Oh, oh

Ilumina o asfalto negro."
Oh, oh"

(Inspired by the song, "Calma" by Marisa Monte)

Performed by: Marisa Monte
Songwriters: Marisa De Azevedo Monte/Francisco Buarque De Freitas

Music is Gonna Save Us

(La Musica ci Salverà)

Do you have the music inside you?
Do you want to dance & sing?
Do you want to do some *"Jive Talkin'"*?
Do you want to do some *"jammin'"*?
Do you want to *"rap"* out?
Do you want to *bust* out?
Do you want to *party the night away*?
Do you want to *Rage ALL night long*?
Do you want to have *FUN*?
Do you want to *FEEL ALIVE?*
Do you want to *BE ALIVE*?
Do you want to FEEL the *ENERGY*?
Do you want to FEEL the *INTENSITY*?
Do you want to FEEL *"The HUMAN"*?
Do you want to FEEL the *MUSIC*?

YES!!!
Well...

Get the music inside you!
Because...
...music is gonna save us!
Yes, you hear me!
Music is gonna save us.
Music is gonna save me.
Music is gonna save you.
Music is gonna save us.

All you have to do is...
...open up.
...let in.
...let it into your HE♥RT.
...let it into your SOUL.
...let it consume you.
...let it swallow you up.

Get the music inside you!
Because...
...music is gonna save us!

Yes, you hear me!
Music is gonna save us.
Music is gonna save me.
Music is gonna save you.
Music is gonna save us.

"Don't EVER let the music inside you DIE!"

"The Don"
16.07.2021

You've Gotta Take What You Get
(Devi Prendere Quello che Ottieni)

You can't refuse.
You can't say no.
You can't complain.
You can't argue.
You can't negotiate.
You can't barter.
You can't discuss it.
You can't want something different.
You've gotta take what you get.

Be thankful for what you're getting.
You might be getting nothing at all.
So don't *quibble*.
Don't be *ungrateful*.
Don't argue.
Don't *whinge*.
Don't *whine*.
Don't be *grumpy*.
Don't be a *sook*.
Don't be a *"cry baby"*.
Don't *sulk*.
You've gotta take what you get.

Be *thankful*.
Be *grateful*.
Be *appreciative*.
Be *gracious*.
Be *accepting*.
Be *humble*.
Be *kind*.
Be *LO♥ING*.
You've gotta take what you get.

"Remember there are people way worse off than you!"

"The Don"
16.07.2021

Don't Ask the Question

(Non Fare la Domanda)

Are you ready for the answer?
Are you prepared for the reply?
Are you okay with what might be said?
Are you fine with the possible response?
Because if you're not...
...don't ask the question.
...if you might not like the answer.

Sometimes it's better not to know.
Sometimes it's better to be blissfully ignorant.
Sometimes it's better to have your head in the clouds.
Sometimes it's better to be *"safe than sorry"*.
Sometimes it's better not to see.
Sometimes it's better not to ask
Sometimes it's better not to ask the question...
...if you might not like the answer.

Let things be.
Don't *"rock the boat"*.
If it's working, why change it?
Go with the flow.
Be fluidic.
Be cool.
Be calm.
Don't get stressed.
Don't get agitated.
If you're happy with your situation...
...it's probably better to leave things as they are.
Don't ask the question, if you might not like the answer!

"I asked the question & I didn't like the answer!"
"I shouldn't have asked the question!"
"Now I'm sorry I did!"

"The Don"
17.07.2021

The day the Universe Changed
(Il Giorno in cui l'Universo è Cambiato)

The day the Universe Changed.
Was the day I was born.
The day you were born.
The day anyone is born.
That's the day the Universe Changed.

The Universe is constantly changing.
The Universe is in constant motion.
The Universe is in constant dynamics.
That's the day the Universe Changed.

We are children of the Universe.
We are made of star stuff.
When we were born the Universe spoke.
That's the day the Universe Changed.

So, don't take your life lightly.
Don't waste it away.
Don't think your life is meaningless.
Because when you were born...
... that's the day the Universe Changed.

"The Don"
17.07.2021

The Perfect Saturday Night

(Il Sabato Sera Perfetto di Sempre)

It was a GREAT Saturday night
It started with her bring sauce.
Then the red wine was requested for.
Then the pasta.
Penne, of course.
What a Saturday night.
The Best Saturday Night
The Perfect Saturday Night.

Whilst this was boiling.
She played on the piano.
All from memory.
She has an AMAZING memory.
What a Saturday night.
The Best Saturday Night
The Perfect Saturday Night.

"Oh, what a night!"
"It was the PERFECT Saturday night!"

"Another Saturday night and I ain't got nobody
I got some money 'cause i just got paid
How I wish I had someone to talk to
I'm in an awful way.

I got in town a month ago, I seen a lotta girls since then
If I could meet 'em I could get 'em but as yet I haven't met 'em
That's why I'm in the shape I'm in.

Here another Saturday night and I ain't got nobody
I got some money 'cause I just got paid
How I wish I had someone to talk to
I'm in an awful way.

Another fella told me he had a sister who looked just fine
Instead of being my deliverance, she had a strange resemblance
To a cat named Frankenstein.

Another Saturday night and I ain't got nobody
I got some money 'cause I just got paid
How I wish I had some someone to talk to
I'm in an awful way (one more time)."

"Another Saturday night and I ain't got nobody
I got some money 'cause I just got paid
How I wish I had some someone to talk to
I'm in an awful way (one more time)."

Here's another Saturday night and I ain't got nobody
I got some money 'cause I just got paid
How I wish I had some chick to talk to
I'm in an awful way.

Here it is another weekend and I ain't got nobody
Man, if I was back home I'd be swinging
Two chicks on my arm
Aww yeah
Listen to me huh.

It's hard on a fella, when he don't know his way around
If I don't find me a honey to help me spend my money
I'm gonna have to blow this town.

Here it's another Saturday night and I ain't got nobody
I got some money 'cause I just got paid
How I wish I had some chick to talk to
I'm in an awful way (everybody sing)."

Songwriter: Sam Cooke

"The Don"
18.07.2021

I Am in Prison

(Sono in Prigione)

My eyes are bleeding.
My veins are boiling.
What have they done with Liberty?
My of days on the beach.
My walks in the forest.
And my eyes looking at the mountains through the sky.
What of all these things if I cannot come & go?
I am a prisoner.
I am in Prison.

I'm caught in this net.
I'm caught & I can't escape.
There is no way out.
There is no escape.
I wanna get out of here.
This is a *"Living HELL"!*
I am a prisoner.
I am in Prison.

"The Don"/Miriam
18.07.2021

Why?

Perché?

Why?

"The Don"
19.07.2021

Where the Streets Have No Names
(Dove le Strade Non Hanno Nome)

There is darkness everywhere.
There is pestilence in the air.
There are dark clouds in the sky.
There is a darkness inside the town...
...where the streets have no names.

There is no one about.
The streets are deserted.
The ghosts have come out to play.
They are no longer lurking in the shadows.
They don't have to.
In the town...
...where the streets have no names.

The children are hiding under their beds.
Their parents are riddled with fear.
They are living in terror.
There is nothing they can do about it.
The FASCISTS have WON.
In the town...
...where the streets have no names.

"The Don"
19.07.2021

Be Shameless

(Senza Vergogna)

Be ridiculous.
Be crazy.
Be unrestricted.
Be weird.
Be insane.
Be a looney.
Be frivolous
Be zany.
Be whacky.
Be brazen.
Be carefree.
Be wild.
Be rebellious.
Be yourself.
Be whomever you want to be.
Be CrEaTiVe.
Be WONDERFUL.
Be ALIVE.
Be SHAMELESS!

"Have NO shame!"
"Be SHAMELESS!"

"The Don"
20.07.2021

Come in From the Cold

(Vieni dal Freddo)

It's blowing a gale.
It's a hurricane a blowin'.
It's freezing out there.
It's wild & wooly.
It's tempestuous & treacherous.
It's raining *"cats & dogs"*.
It's pissing down.
It's cataclysmic.
It's thunderous.
It's dangerous.
It's Armageddon.
It's the *"End of the World"*.
It's the *"End of Time"*.
It's the "*End of Days."*
It's time to get out of the rain.
It's time to seek shelter from the storm.
It's time to come out of the cold.
It's time to come in from the cold.

"It's nice & warm in here!"
"It's safe in here!"
"The log fire is raging"
"We can have some mulled wine!"

It's time to come in from the cold.

"The Don"
20.07.2021

Do you Have the Courage?
(Hai il Coraggio?)

Do you have the courage to stand up for what you believe in?
Do you have the courage to put you actions where you mouth is?
Do you have the courage to put your life on the line?
Do you have the courage to protest?
Do you have the courage to rebel against the System!
Do you have the courage to rebel against the Establishment?
Do you have the courage to rage against The Machine?
Do you have the courage?

Do you have the courage to storm the Bastille?
Do you have the courage to put a flower into the nozzle of a policeman's gun?
Do you have the courage to stand defiantly in front of a Chinese military tank?
Do you have the courage stand up for your rights?
Do you have the courage to march on the streets?
Do you have the courage to rebel against the System!
Do you have the courage to rebel against the Establishment?
Do you have the courage to rage against The Machine?
Do you have the courage?

Do you have the guts?

Do you have the courage?

Do you have the courage?

"The Don"
21.07.2021

Calm Your Mind

(Calma la tua Mente)

You think too much.
You have too much noise inside your head.
You've gotta *turn it off.*
You've gotta *shut it down.*
You've gotta *calm your mind.*

You stress too much.
You overthink.
You worry about...
...the Future.
...the Past.
...the Present.
You've gotta calm your mind.

Relax.
Chill out.
Chillax.
Meditate.
Fornicate.
Masturbate.
But whatever you do...
...you must calm your mind.

"I get HIGH!"
"That works for me!"
"Try it, it might work for you too!"

"The Don"
22.07.2021

Got you on My Mind
(Ti ho nella Mia Mente)

You're always on my mind.
You're always in my head.
But it's okay...
...I've learnt to live with it.
...I've learnt to deal with it.
...I've learnt to handle it.
...over time anyway.
Because...
...I've always got you on my mind.

It's not a bad thing.
I've learnt to accept it.
I've learnt to live with it.
There's no point fighting it.
There's no point struggling with it.
"It is what it is!"
I've always got you on my mind.

"Except when I'm sleeping!"
"I don't dream about you though!"

*"I've got you on my mind
I'm feeling kind of sad and low
Got you on my mind
Feeling kind of sad and low
I'm wondering where you are
Wondering why you had to go.*

*Tears begin to fall
Every time I hear your name
Tears begin to fall
Every time I hear your name
But since you went away
Nothing seems to be the same."*

"I've got you on my mind
I'm feeling kind of sad and low
Feeling kind of sad and low
I'm wondering where you are
Wondering why you had to go.

No matter how I try
I can't forget you
If ever it should be
You want to come back to me
You know I'd let you.

I've got you on my mind
I'm feeling kind of sad and low
Got you on my mind
Feeling kind of sad and low
I'm wondering where you are
Wondering why you had to go."

Performed by: Eric Clapton
Songwriters: Joe Thomas/Howard Biggs

"The Don"
22.07.2021

WANTED DEAD OR ALIVE

(Ricercato VIVO o MORTO)

For crimes against Humanity.
Crimes committed include being...
...kind.
...caring.
...compassionate.
...respectful.
...fair.
...reasonable.
...forgiving.
...empathetic.
...affectionate.
...social.
...HAPPY.
...LO❤ING.

"There are other crimes too "heinous" to be listed, to spare the minds of young children & the elderly from permanent psychological trauma!"

Wanted DEAD or ALIVE!
"Preferably DEAD!"
"He talks too much!"
"Another crime we didn't mention."

"I'm a very naughty little boy!"

"He's a very naughty little boy!"

"The Don"
22.07.2021

Why not?

(Perchè No?)

Why not?

"The Don"
22.07.2021

Happiness

(Oh Lord, Won't you Buy Me a Mercedes Benz)
(Felicità (Oh Signore non mi Comprerai una Mercedes Benz))

Happiness is an *internal* condition.
It is not determined by *external* factors.
You carry it around inside you.
Independent of the things happening outside around you.
Happiness is not dependant on the acquisition of material objects.
Such as...
...*money.*
...*fame.*
...*power.*
...*sex.*
...*LO♥E.*

Happiness is *NOT a warm gun.*
Happiness is a *state of mind.*
Happiness is a *way of being.*
Happiness is *internal.*
Happiness is *inside you.*
Happiness is *internal freedom.*
Happiness is *internal peace.*

Happiness cannot be *bought.*
Happiness cannot be *sold.*
Happiness cannot be *manufactured.*
Happiness cannot be *faked.*
Happiness cannot be *copied.*
Happiness cannot be *reproduced.*
Happiness cannot be *found.*

Marriage cannot give you happiness.
Family cannot bring you happiness.
Children cannot give you happiness.
Security cannot bring you happiness.
Religion cannot bring you happiness.
God cannot give you happiness.
No one else can give you happiness.
Nothing else can bring you happiness.

Only you can give yourself happiness.
Because...
...happiness comes from within you.
...happiness comes from inside you.

"Oh lord won't you buy me a Mercedes Benz.
My friends all drive Porsches, I must make amends.
Worked hard all my lifetime, no help from my friends.
So, oh lord won't you buy me a Mercedes Benz.

Oh lord won't you buy me a colour TV.
Dialing for dollars is trying to find me.
I wait for delivery each day until 3.
So, oh lord won't you buy me a colour TV.

Oh lord won't you buy me a night on the town.
I'm counting on you lord, please don't let me down.
Prove that you love me and buy the next round.
Oh lord, won't you buy me a night on the town.

Oh lord won't you buy me a Mercedes Benz
My friends all drive Porsches, I must make amends.
Worked hard all my lifetime, no help from my friends.
So, oh lord won't you buy me a Mercedes Benz."

Performed by: Janis Joplin
Songwriters: Janis Joplin/ Bob Neuwirth/Michael McClure

"The Don"
23.07.2021

I Can't **STOP** Myself

(Io Non Mi Posso Fermare)

I've been told to **"STOP"** many times.
I go *"too far"*.
I know.
But sometimes I just get carried away.
I have to express myself.
I've gotta express my feelings.
And I go *"too far"*.
"STOP"!

I try VERY hard to *refrain*.
I try VERY hard to *"hold back"*.
I try VERY hard to *"control myself.*
I try VERY hard to *"withdraw"*.
I try VERY hard to *"reign"* myself in.
I try VERY hard to **"STOP"!**

I know the outcome.
I know the answer.
I know what's gonna happen.
I know the conclusion.
I know the ending.
When I don't...
...**"STOP"!**

There is no *epilogue*.
There is no *"happy ending'*.
There is no *"happy ever after*.
There is no *"pot of gold at the end of the rainbow"*.
When I don't...
...**"STOP"!**

"The Don"
23.07.2021

STOP!
(Fermare!)

STOP!

"The Don"
24.07.2021

Don't Worry, Be Happy
(Non Preoccuparti, Sii Felice)

Don't worry, be happy!

"The Don"
24.07.2021

Freedom (What Freedom?)
(Libertà (quale libertà?))

I don't know what that word means anymore.
Everybody's going crazy.
There is madness in the air.
It's a *contagion*.
It's *making everybody go insane*.
It's an *endemic*.
It's a *pandemic*.
It's *systemic*.
It's *problematic*.
It's *symptomatic*.
It's *pathetic*.

Don't *laugh*.
Don't *sing*.
Don't *dance*.
Don't *party*.
Don't *rage*.
Don't *fart*.
Don't *shit*.
Don't *FUCK*.
Don't *rebel*.
Don't *question*.
Don't *protest*.

DON'T.

Just...
...*DON'T.*

"You can't, even if you wanted to!"
"Freedom...
... what Freedom?"
"There is no Freedom!"

"Just ACCEPT!"

"Freedom...
... what Freedom?"

"The Don"
24.07.2021

DON'T!
(Non Farlo)

DON'T!

"The Don"
24.07.2021

ACCEPT!
(Acceto)

ACCEPT!

"The Don"
24.07.2021

FASCISM HAS WON!

(Il Fascismo ha Vinto!)

"It's time to cry!"

FASCISM HAS WON!

"Now is the time for your tears!

"The Don"
24.07.2021

Watch & See

(Guadare e Vedere)

Watch this space.
Stay tuned.
It's not over till it's over.
Let it play out till the end.
Don't come to any conclusions.
Don't get excited.
Don't start making plans.
Stay calm.
Just...
...*watch & see.*

See yourself seated on the bench where you always felt you belonged.
See yourself on a swing where you always feel secure.
See yourself floating on the water.
See what feeds your SOUL.

"The Don"/Miriam
24.07.2021

Don't FUCK Around with ME!
(Non Scopare in Giro con ME!)

You've crossed the line.
Just...
... don't!

Don't FUCK Around with ME!

"The Don"/Miriam
24.07.2021

Deconstruct

(Decostruire)

Deconstruct...

...to

Reconstruct.

"The Don"
24.07.2021

No Words Required

(Non Parole e Necessaria)

No words needed.
No need to speak.
No need to say a thing.
No need to open your mouth.
No need to make a sound.
It's completely understood.
Because there are...
...no words required.

It's silent communication.
It's nothing you need to say.
It's already transmitted.
It's already received.
It's a look.
It's a gesture.
Because there are...
...no words required.

What needs to be said is said.
What needs to be done is done.
What needs to be understood is understood.
What needs to be confirmed is confirmed.
What needs to be made clear is made clear.
What needs to be resolved is resolved.
Because there are...
...no words required.

"The Don"
25.07.2021

PROTEST!

(Protesta)

It's your democratic right.
It's your human right.
To...

... PROTEST!

"Don't let it be taken away from you!"

"Always responsibly, of course!"

"The Don"
26.07.2021

Hypocrisy

(Ipocrisia)

"Do what I SAY, NOT what I DO!"

"Hypocrite!"

"Hypocrisy is rampant!"

"The Don"
26.07.2021

I Do Whatever the FUCK I Want!
(Faccio Tutto il CAZZO che Voglio)

I say whatever the FUCK I want!
I think whatever the FUCK I want!
I don't care what the FUCK you think.
I don't SEEK your approval.
I don't NEED your approval.
I do whatever the FUCK I want!

"*Always responsibly, of course!*"

"The Don"
26.07.2021

Ghost Town

(Città Fantasma)

It's nothing but a *"Ghost Town!"*
There's no one around.
This place is a *"Ghost Town"!*

"It must be the end of the World!"

*"This town (town) is coming like a ghost town
All the clubs have been closed down
This place (town) is coming like a ghost town
Bands won't play no more
Too much fighting on the dance floor.*

*Do you remember the good old days before the ghost town?
We danced and sang, and the music played in a de boomtown.*

*This town (town) is coming like a ghost town
Why must the youth fight against themselves?
Government leaving the youth on the shelf
This place (town) is coming like a ghost town
No job to be found in this country
Can't go on no more
The people getting angry.*

*This town is coming like a ghost town
This town is coming like a ghost town
This town is coming like a ghost town
This town is coming like a ghost town."*

Songwriter: Jerry Dammers
Performed by: The Specials

"The Don"
26.07.2021

Fuck Like Animals

(Scopa Come gli Animali)

We ARE animals!
So, let's fuck like animals!
Don't *hold back*.
Don't be *shy*.
Don't be *inhibited*.
Don't have any *inhibitions*.
Let's fuck like animals.

Let's be *primitive*.
Let's be *feral*.
Let's be *savage*.
Let's be *tribal*.
Let's be *wild*.
Let's be *untamed*.
Let's be *undomesticated*.
Let's be *uncivilized*.
Let's fuck like animals.

Let's get *on all fours*.
Let's get *on the floor*.
Let's go *to the jungle*.
Let's *climb up the trees*.
Let's *swing on the vines*.
Let's *be naked & free*.
Let's *do it everywhere*.
Let's fuck like animals.

"You let me violate you
You let me desecrate you
You let me penetrate you
You let me complicate you.

Help me; I broke apart my insides
Help me; I've got no soul to sell
Help me; the only thing that works for me
Help me get away from myself.

I wanna fuck you like an animal
I wanna feel you from the inside
I wanna fuck you like an animal
My whole existence is flawed.

You get me closer to God
You can have my isolation; you can have the hate that it brings
You can have my absence of faith; you can have my everything.

Help me tear down my reason
Help me; it's your sex I can smell
Help me; you make me perfect
Help me become somebody else.

I wanna fuck you like an animal
I wanna feel you from the inside
I wanna fuck you like an animal
My whole existence is flawed.

You get me closer to God
Through every forest, above the trees
Within my stomach, scraped off my knees
I drink the honey inside your hive
You are the reason I stay alive."

"Closer"- Performed by: Nine Inche Nails
Songwriter: Reznor Michael Trent

"The Don"
27.07.2021

DON'T STAY SAFE

(Non Stare Al Sicuro)

What the fuck does that mean?
Stay safe!
No!
I will NOT stay *"safe"*!
I am not going to take your advice.
Thanks all the same.
But I am not going to stay *"safe"*.

I'm going to be reckless.
I'm going to be outrageous.
I'm going to be wild.
I'm going to be frivolous.
But I am not going to stay *"safe"*.

I'm going to party.
I'm going to rage.
I'm going to dance.
I'm going to sing.
I'm going to socialise.
I'm going to fuck.
I'm going to LIVE!
I'm not going to stay *"safe"*.

" LIVE your life!"
"Don't waste it away by staying "safe."

" Don't stay safe!"

"The Don"
27.07.2021

TROUBLE MAKER

(Piantagrane)

I'm a trouble maker.
I make trouble everywhere I go.
I am rude.
I am crude.
I use foul language.
I swear a lot.
I am shameless.
I have no shame.
Because...
...I am a trouble maker.

Stay out of my way.
I'll make trouble for you.
I'll take the piss out of you.
I have no limits.
I'll say things I shouldn't say.
I'll say words such as...
...fuck.
...cunt.
...pussy.
...twat.
...cock.
...arsehole.
Why?
Because I like to.
Because...
...I am a trouble maker.

I'll tell you things you don't want to hear.
I'll make jokes out of things that are not supposed to be funny.
I'll be sacrilegious.
I'll be blasphemous.
I'll even make fun of God.

I'll say such things as...
..."*do you know that God spelt backwards is "Dog"?*"
I'll make fun of the Irish.
I'll make fun of the Scottish.
I'll make fun of the *"Bloody Poms", (the English for those unfamiliar with that term)*.
I'll make fun of the *"Aussies", (the Australians for those unfamiliar with that term)*.
Why?
Because I like to.
Because...
...I am a trouble maker.

I even make fun of life.
I don't take life seriously.
I'll tell you that *"Life is a joke!"*
I'll tell you to *"lighten up"*!
I'll tell you that you have *"no sense of humour"*!
I'll be ruthless.
I don't know when to stop.
Because...
...I am a trouble maker.

You'll probably think that I'm crazy!
But that's alright because I don't care!
I do whatever the FUCK I want!
Why?
Because I like to.
Because...
...I am a trouble maker.

If you're looking for trouble...
... you've come to the right place.
Call me *"Trouble"*...
... *"Trouble Maker!"*
Why?
Because I like to.

Because...
...I am a trouble maker.

"If you're looking for trouble
You came to the right place
If you're looking for trouble
Just look right in my face
I was born standing up
And talking back
My daddy was a green-eyed mountain jack.

Because I'm evil, my middle name is misery (yeah, yeah)
Well, I'm evil, so don't you mess around with me.

I've never looked for trouble
But I've never ran
I don't take no orders
From no kind of man
I'm only made out
Of flesh, blood and bone
But if you're gonna start a rumble
Don't you try it on alone.

Because I'm evil, my middle name is misery
Well, I'm evil, so don't you mess around with me.

I'm evil, evil, evil, as can be
I'm evil, evil, evil, as can be
So don't mess around, don't mess around, don't mess around with me
I'm evil, I'm evil, evil, evil
So don't mess around, don't mess around with me
I'm evil, I tell you I'm evil
So don't mess around with me
Yeah!"

Songwriters: "Trouble"-Leiber Jerry/Stoller Mike
Performed by: Elvis Presley

"The Don"
28.07.2021

Remember, You Can Do Anything!
(Ricorda, Puoi Fare Qualsiasi Cosa!)

A mother on her deathbed.
The last time she saw her daughter.
They say their goodbyes.
She knows she is going to die.
This will be the last time they will see each other.
These are her last words to her daughter…
…*"Remember, you can do anything!"*

What will your last words be?
When you are about to *"exit stage left"*?
When the final curtain falls?
When you *"shuffle off your mortal coil"*?
When you take your last breath?
What *"pearls of wisdom"* will you utter?
Maybe they will be...
…*"Remember, you can do anything!"*

"The last words from a mother to her daughter."

Dedicated to "Marie Ethel Gardner"

"The Don"
28.07.2021

Narcissist

(Narcisista)

"You are a narcissist!"
Am I a narcissist?
Are you a narcissist?
A narcissist is someone who only thinks about themselves.
"Well, hello, that's just about everyone in the whole world!"

I LO♥E myself, that's true.
But do I LO♥E myself too much?
Anyway, how much is too much?
Am I self-obsessed?
Am I self-indulgent?
Am I self-centred?
Am I selfish?
Am I a Narcissist?
Possibly!

But who isn't?

But I do LO♥E myself!

"Is that bad?"

"The Don"
28.07.2021

Voice of the Voiceless

(La Voce dei Senza Voce)

Who'll speak for the *shadows?*
Who'll speak for the *ghosts?*
Who'll speak for the *anonymous?*
Who'll speak for the *invisible?*
Who'll speak for the *downtrodden?*
Who'll speak for the *homeless?*
Who'll speak for the *poor?*
Who'll speak for the *abused?*
Who'll speak for the *discriminated?*
Who'll speak for the *persecuted?*
Who'll speak for the *oppressed?*
Who'll speak for the *outcasts?*
Who'll speak for the *young?*
Who'll speak for the *old?*
Who'll speak for the voiceless?

I am the voice of the voiceless.
I am an anthem for the voiceless.
I will speak for the voiceless.
I will be the voice of the voiceless.
I will be the mouthpiece for the voiceless.
I will shout for the voiceless.
I will scream for the voiceless.
I will be the voice of the voiceless!

Will you join me?
Will you be a voice for the voiceless?
I can't do this on my own.
Many voices a choir make!
Let's ALL become voices for the voiceless!

"The Don"
28.07.2021

What Sort of Death Will You Have?
(Che Tipo di Morte Avrai?)

As my father lay dying in a hospital bed.
I saw the real person come out.
He lay in a state of delirium.
Oscillating between consciousness & semi-consciousness.
Everything that was inside him was free to come out.
All his demons.
All his venom.
All his fears.
All his frustrations.
He no longer could contain them.
What Sort of Death Will you have?

My father did not have a *"good"* death.
He battled till the very end.
He fought very hard.
He was in turmoil.
I guess he had to...
...make things right...
...put things straight.
...clear his conscience.
...make peace with himself.
...let things go.
...reconcile with his actions.
Before he could move on.
What Sort of Death Will you have?

But he didn't have much time.
Time was running out.
He had too much inside him that he let out.
He just let it out to anyone that was there.
It was like a tsunami of emotions.
There was so much darkness inside him.
There was so much venom.
There was so much bile.
There was so much torment.

My father was not a happy man in Life.
My father was not a happy man in Death.
My father did not have a happy Death.
What Sort of Death Will you have?

I sat by his side & watched him struggling with his demons.
They had come back to taunt him.
They had waited till he was weak.
They had waited till the time was right.
They had waited patiently until their time was ready.
They had waited until he was on his *"Deathbed"*.
Then they awoke.
He was defenseless.
He didn't stand a chance.
He was FUCKED!
My father died a miserable Death.
What Sort of Death Will you have?

I saw it all.
I was there.
I could do nothing but watch him struggling, fighting, losing his battles.
Until it was all over.
He had taken his last breath.
He was DEAD.
He had lost.
The demons had won.
What Sort of Death Will you have?

Have a *"good"* LIFE so that you can have a *"good"* DEATH!

My father did not have a good DEATH.
What Sort of Death Will you have?

"The Don"
29.07.2021

Eco-Warrior

(Eco-Guerriero)

Who fights for the Earth?
Are you an *"Eco-Warrior"*?
Do you fight for planet Earth?
Are you it's protector?
Or...
... *it's "Destroyer"?*
Which side do you belong to?
Are you an "Eco-Warrior"?

Will you defend planet Earth?
Will you stand up & protect its fragile ecosystem?
Will you fight for the habits of endangered animals?
Will you protest the cutting down of native rainforests?
Will you actively engage in political campaigns to support action on climate change?
Will you become political & force politicians to legislate for the protection of our natural environment?
Will you become an "Eco-Warrior"?

"Ghia needs your help!"

"The Don"
29.07.2021

What Kind of Drunk Are You?
(Che Tipo di Ubriaco Sei?)

What kind of drunk are you?
A "happy" drunk?
A "miserable" drunk?
An "abusive" drunk?
A "violent" drunk?
What kind of drunk are you?

Whichever one you are...
...everything is inside of you.
It's all there already.
...waiting to come out.
Being drunk is just the key that opens the door.
The door that is normally kept shut tight.
But when the floodgates are opened...
...then they all come pouring out.
There is no controlling these emotions.
There is nothing to stop them.
They are free to do what they please.
What kind of drunk are you?

Luckily, I'm a "happy" drunk.
What kind of drunk are you?

"The Don"
29.07.2021

When There is No Tomorrow
(Quando non c'è Domani)

That's the final hurdle.
Do not fuck around with other issues.
Don't be side-tracked by superfluous trivialities.
Focus on the *"main game"*.
The *"End play"*.
Control this.
Stand in front of it.
Face it.
Look at its eyes.
Look into its eyes.
Stare it down.
Are you capable?
Are you strong enough?
Do you have the...
...*"staying power"*?
...the *"mental aptitude"*?
When you are confronted with the fact that...
...*there is no tomorrow!*

Can you cope?
What will you do?
Will you...
...*panic?*
...*freeze up?*
...*piss yourself?*
...*shit you pants?*
...*stand in TERROR?*
...*confront the challenge?*
...*put up a fight?*
...*conquer your DEMONS?*
...*walk on through to the "Other Side"?*
When there is no tomorrow!

"Look at the "Big Picture"!"

"The Don"
29.07.2021

Boundaries

(Confini)

Boundaries?
What boundaries?
There are no *boundaries*.
There are no *borders*.
There are no *countries*.
There are no *nations*.
There are no *rules*.
There are no *laws*.
There are no *roads*.
There are no *religions*.
There are no *Devils*.
There are no *Gods*.
There are no *limits*.
There are no boundaries.

There is no *justice*.
There is no *legal system*.
There is no *political system*.
There is no *financial system*.
There is no *monetary system*.
There is no *money*.
There is no *government*.
There is no *"System"*.
There is no *"Establishment"*.
There is no *limit*.
There is no boundary.

There are no limits.
There are no boundaries.

It's all *FAKE!*
It's all an *ILLUSION*.
It's all *"Man-made"*.

There are no limits.
There are no boundaries.

"The Don"
30.07.2021

Time

(Tempo)

Time is such a mysterious entity.

Time can *go fast*.
Time can *go slow*.
Time can *move forwards*.
Time can *move backwards*.
Time can *"stand still"*.
Time doesn't exist.

There's *"Space-Time"*.
There's the *"Space-Time Continuum"*.
There's a *"Rift in Time"*.
There's a *"Stitch in Time saves nine"*.
There's *"Outside of Time"*.
There's *"Time Dilation"*.
There's a *"Time when it all began"*.
There's the *"Beginning of Time"*.
There's the *"End of Time"*.
There's *"Time is running out"*.
There's *"Your Time is just beginning"*.
There's *"Your Time hasn't come yet"*.
There's *"Your Time is over"*.
There's *"You're out of Time"*.

There's *"the Place that Time forgot"*.
There's *"Time is money"*.
There's *"I've got Time to kill"*.

Time is all over the place.
It's not the *"Right Time"*.
It was not the *"Right Time"*
It's the *"Wrong Time"*.
It was the "*Wrong Time"*.
Lost *"In Time"*.
I wish you would come "On Time"!

You're just *"In Time"*!
You've *"Run out of Time"*!
It's not *"My Time"* yet.
"Time is on my side".
"Does anybody really know what Time it is?"
I think it's *"Wine O'clock!"*
"Time keeps on slipping into the Future!"

"My Time is over!"
"Give me some more Time!"
"Time is running out!"
"Quick, there's "no Time" to lose!"
There's *"NO Time Left!"*

Some claim that *Time doesn't exist.*
That it's just an *"Illusion"*.
"So, WTF have I been doing ALL this Time?"
Has my Life been just a *"Waste of Time"*?
"By the way, what time is it?"
"I think I've spent "Too much Time" here!"
"Time stops for no one!"
"It's Time for me to go!"

"The Don"
30.07.2021

FOLLOW THE RULES!
(Segui le Regole)

FOLLOW THE
RULES!

"Don't follow the RULES!"

"The Don"
30.07.2021

Cover artwork for:
"Poems for the Outsiders, Displaced, Dispossessed, Discarded & Unwanted"
Published: 10th Sept, 2021
Book of Poems 14
Artist: Daniela Dali (Insta: artbysdaniela)

Books written by "The Don"

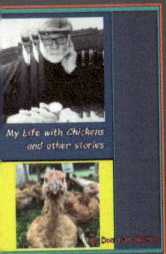

"My Life with Chickens & other stories: I Pity the Poor Immigrant"
Published:
10th September, 2019
Autobiography Book 1:
0 – 12 years old

"Poems for Misfits, Miscreants, Misanthropes, Mavericks, Losers & Malcontents!"
Published:
10th June, 2020
Book of Poems 1

"Poems for Troubled Minds & Trouble Hearts"
Published:
10th August, 2020
Book of Poems 2

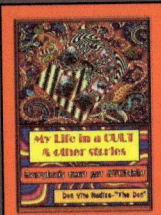

"My Life in a CULT & other stories: Everybody Must Get STONED!"
Published:
10th September, 2020
Autobiography Book 2:
15 – 30 years old

"Poems for Restless Minds & Restless Hearts"
Published:
10th October, 2020
Book of Poems 3

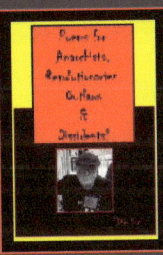

"Poems for Anarchists, Revolutionaries, Outlaws & Dissidents!"
Published:
10th November, 2020
Book of Poems 4

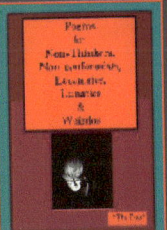

"Poems for Non-Thinkers & Eccentrics"
Published:
10th December, 2020
Book of Poems 5

"The Rantings of a Madman"
Published:
10th January, 2021
Book of Poems 6

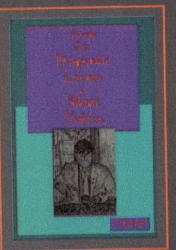

"Poems for Desperate Lovers & Silent Voices"
Published:
10th February, 2021
Book of Poems 7

"Poems for Tormented Minds & Tortured Souls"
Published:
10th March, 2021
Book of Poems 8

All available ONLY online

Books written by "The Don"

"Poems for ALIENS, Outsiders, Outcasts & other STRANGE BEINGS!"
Published: 10th April, 2021
Book of Poems 9

"Poems for Beings From Another Planet"
Published: 10th May, 2021
Book of Poems 10

"Poems for Mindless Beings & Lost Souls"
Published: 10th June, 2021
Book of Poems 11

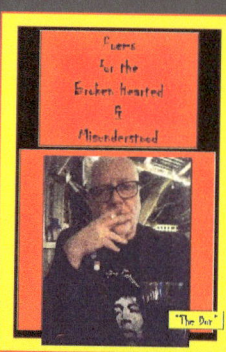

"Poems for the Broken Hearted & Misunderstood
Published: 10th July, 2021
Book of Poems 12

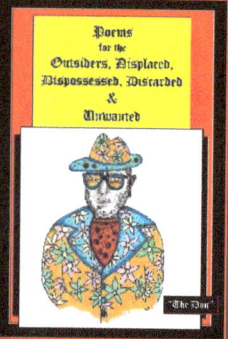

"Poems for Poems for the Bewildered, Dazed & Confused"
10th August, 2021

Book of Poems 13

"Poems for the Outsiders, Displaced, Dispossessed, Discarded & Unwanted"
Published: 10th Sept, 2021
Book of Poems 14

All available ONLY online

"Poems for Secret Agents, Phantom Agents, Agents of Change, Agent Provocateurs & Agents of Chaos"
Published: 10th Oct, 2021
Book of Poems 15

Vito Radice ("The Don")
(Poet/Author/Polemicist/Non-Thinker/Non-Intellectual)
Email: vitoradice@gmail.com
Instagram: don_vito_radice
Facebook: Vito Radice
Mobile: +61490012461
(Australia)

www.ingramcontent.com/pod-product-compliance
Lightning Source LLC
Chambersburg PA
CBHW042048290426
44109CB00006B/146